Mellifluous

by

K.P. Anderson

UnCollected Press

Mellifluous

Cover Image Sources:

Thistle from plate 60, "A Scottish Thistle" in Thorburn, Archibald, 1860-1935. *A Naturalist's Sketch Book.* London: Longmans, Green and co., 1919. Digitized and presented at the Biodiversity Heritage Library (BHL).

Bee from *The Story of a Picture.* New York: J. Ottmann Lithographing, 1893. https://archive.org/details/storyofpicture00newy/page/n3/mode/2up.

Parchment background by Caleb Kimbrough from https://commons.wikimedia.org/wiki/File:Parchment.00.jpg https://www.flickr.com/photos/calebkimbrough/4691644631.

Book Design by:

UnCollected Press
8320 Main Street, 2nd Floor
Ellicott City, MD 21043

For more books by UnCollected Press:
www.therawartreview.com

First Edition 2022
ISBN: 978-1-7378731-2-9

This book is dedicated to those who bring abundance into the world and to those in need of it

CONTENTS

MATING FLIGHT / 1

LABOR / 2

LARVAL IMPRESSION / 4

METAMORPHOSIS / 5

COME, SISTERS, / 6

LAMENTATION OF DRONES / 7

WINTER CLUSTER / 8

ORIENTATION FLIGHTS / 9

FORAGE DANCES / 10

THE PLUNDERED / 11

COLLAPSE / 12

CODA / 13

MATING FLIGHT

The only time she flew
She was drawn along the flyways
By that hook in the belly,
That fluorescent sense of
The core, a rising map,
A moment's flux
Leading her to
The camber of a slope that fit
Instinctively behind her eyes
Confirming the composition
Of scent and sparring
Harmonics pitched
A half-scale up from the wind

Trees, sediment, sunlight, site
All inclined to her arrival, roused
The drones, funneled their flight
Steered them towards
The rite that they were fashioned for
And she, bedeviling the crosscurrent,
Accepted their sacrifice

Marked with the future
She returned, pausing once
On a roof slate
To watch the afternoon
Cant the camellias
Years of wax,
Eggs, honey, hive
Hummed insistent
Tender in her ducts
The shadow of her fragrance
Shifted: expectation
An emblem of the urge
She embodied
Of the possibility she had become

LABOR

chewed to geometric
regularity
the cells tick out
immeasurably

tongues flick
heedful at my setae
antennae rummage for
a token of my vigor

here's a larger cavity
so I place a drone
there is nothing to think of
but the effort

and when the chamber's full
there is always another
sheet of wax
another gleaming box

another minder multiplied
fortifying me to lay –
churn my whole self out
twice-over in a day

how strange that when
every bit's been used
I'm still actual
abdomen quaking

how strange that I
still mark the dancers' beat
articulate my legs
to count off miles

try to catch
from a worker's basket
a molecule of air
for the blush of its aroma

burst vitrine of
the outside world
memory of sun and flight
a longing

for a purpose past
vague intimation
of a self
I can no longer summon

LARVAL IMPRESSION

A different temper of twilight
Liminal
Succulent pressure
Replenished
Ambrosia-fed
I wonder
Floating
Until I grow secure
Replete against the cradle
Mantle advent, a promise
Incomprehensible but certain

METAMORPHOSIS

You may think it a matter
Of minor alteration
Paired ruptures at the surface
And triumph unfurls

That my time encased served as
Respite in a chamber built
For devotion, furnished with
The foretaste of grace

When all efforts break airborne
You may ignore the ballast
Transition's dim shudder as
My tissues dissolved

In their own juices, betrayed
By mute instinct, accompliced
To destruction, and never
Comprehending why

COME, SISTERS,

Let us become our own scaffold
Leg to leg
Assemble

Fix this cavern to flourish
Sculpt it to thrive
Only when our heat

Has shaped a hive
May you aspire to entrain
Your own calling

LAMENTATION OF DRONES

Just how could we have known
What stagnant fall would bring
With summer's promise blown
The thorns fade, chalked as bone –
No inkling left of spring
Just how could we have known
That once the brood had grown
Fond comb would turn to sting
With summer's promise blown
Our sisters' tempers hone
Their eyes, our reckoning
Just how could we have known
Warmth can be overthrown
And mangled like a wing
With summer's promise blown
We're drowned in grass, alone
Relinquished, wondering
With summer's promise blown
Just how could we have known

WINTER CLUSTER

In mid-November
Dilute sky washes shadow
Alike over brick and branch

Ginkgo leaves – skirts piped
Golden with retreat – glance down
Considering soil

Out back, the beehive
Relaxes splinters from its
Cedar joints, falling dormant

Divulging now and
Then a bee scrambling through
The metal-cast guard

Off to strip the last
Redolent sips of nectar
Outpacing the coming frost

By sunset she will
Retrace the polarized light
Homeward past lampposts

Past catmint, past the
Rose with its second-bud bloom
To alight provisioned for

The shivering time
Ascending through comb, sustained
With recollection

Issuing sweetly
A cloistered hum, the sole sign
Of her thriving heart waiting

ORIENTATION FLIGHTS

We incorporate
Ochre angles, waft beacons
Savor landscapes of return

FORAGE DANCES

Serendipity and sky
And not too strong a breeze

Over where corollas point
To sparks of sweetness

Vitality will leap into your baskets
A few degrees past noon

Fly with me to sip
The laden flowers

Their heads will tip to us
Their lovestruck petals lean

Be swayed by my footfalls
There is so much to be gleaned

Someone come and take this bounty
I am full to bursting with abundance

THE PLUNDERED

Comfort spills sunlit out
Across the vacant doorstep
Replaced by paltry
Granules of gloam
Chafed wood
And yes
Intruder scent
A resin edge which
Saturates the passageways
Infiltrates sense
Roars with its unwelcome wings
Tunes our bodies to its bow
We are spun stark
A remnant clot of honey
Suspended on the wire mesh
Wax chambers torn
The rest –
Our stores, our sisters' summers –
Ransacked
Our future guzzled
Our restoration
Seized to furnish theirs

COLLAPSE

My sisters have dressed the raspberries
My sisters have dressed the wax
My family has dressed the hive
From emergence to emergence

We have scoured our birth bodies
We have scoured cocoons from brood cells
We have scoured the weak nectar
From come-hither bloom to come-hither bloom

A forager wanders the cupolas
A nursemaid wanders the river
A wax moth wanders the comb
Restore us with fragrance, my mother, my queen

My sisters search for marigolds
My sisters search for north
My family searches for home
Dispossessed to unfathomable wilderness

CODA

Last summer
When the shades eclipsed the day like vellum
Stretched across the entrance to a cave
A bee would rise
Enlisting the sun as her lantern
Blithe she'd cast her shadow on the blind
Tracing one last compass pass
On her way to the riverbank
To search out nectar

Then I would stir
And emerge singing hive songs
Let us go
Let us go
Let us return
Let us return
Crouch to scan the workers
Check pollen hauls
The morning churn of preparation
Restrung my bones in gold

Today my window caught
The shadow of a bee
Who was not mine
My hive is empty
Boxes wrapped in plastic
Wax stored on a cupboard shelf
I cannot bring myself to burn their scent away

Yet there are bees to spin
Bees to forage
Bees to light out swift along the river
To dodge catbirds and importune the flowers
Colonies remain

Sequestered in backyards
Piebald hives abide in garden plots
Rustle cemeteries
Hide screened within rooves' sunken paddocks

Bittersweet
These bees will feed
The fruit of other seasons
And with them
I will sing

Acknowledgements

Many thanks are owed to Katrina Berne for her attention and encouragement, Edwin Anderson, Jr., for his feedback and website assistance, Clarke Bustard for his response to the book and proofreading expertise, Ken Mayer for his editing and cover art collaboration, and Laura Piazza for her help with cover layout. Thank you to Jeremy D. Mayer and Diane Seuss for their professional advice and to Dan Collins for his photography. Yusef Komunyakaa, Louis Bayard, Julia Knowlton, and Terri Kirby Erickson showed me great generosity, gifting me with their time and praise, for which I am deeply thankful. I am also in debt to CTY instructors Kevin Young and Rob Content for introducing me to what poetry can be. I am grateful to the editors at Uncollected Press and Henry G. Stanton in particular for their professional support and faith in my work. Their expertise shepherded this chapbook into being. Finally, I would like to thank Kyle MacLea for his unflagging friendship, support, and counsel. The poems in this book would not exist without his confidence in my writing and his persistent willingness to remind me of it.

"In her gorgeous new chapbook, *Mellifluous*, K.P. Anderson reveals herself to be a honey-tongued poet, inviting us into a realm where the natural world meets human imagination. The poems seem to fly, drinking in language the way bees float and labor to extract sweet nectar. This spare but powerful work of poetry transported me, momentarily, beyond the limits of time and space. I did not expect to be moved so fully by these poems; they blend hope with lamentation in order to encode the mysterious impulse of physical and spiritual creativity. Anderson invites us to feel this impulse fully, saying 'Fly with me to sip/The laden flowers,' and her invitation is impossible to resist."

Julia Caroline Knowlton
Poet and Professor, 2018 Georgia Author of the Year

"What I knew of bees, before reading K.P. Anderson's fine collection, *Mellifluous*, was the pain of their stingers in the soles of my bare feet, and that bees are necessary. Therefore, I am most grateful to this author for taking her readers deep into the hive, allowing us to hear the bees' mellifluous, most intimate songs. From her first poem, 'Mating Flight,' to the last, 'Coda,' I was entirely immersed in the complex, interconnected, and private world of bees in a way I never imagined possible, by a poet who brings the hive to life so completely, one might believe she is their frequent guest. Anderson's knowledge of her subject matter is impressive, but what really wowed me is her ability to describe, with such tender feeling, the secret lives of creatures so vital to our survival, we all ought to know more about them— perhaps even fall a little in love with them. Thanks to K.P. Anderson and lines like, 'A bee would rise/Enlisting the sun as her lantern,' I did."

Terri Kirby Erickson
Author of *A Sun Inside My Chest*

K.P. Anderson's poetry has appeared or is forthcoming in *Strong Verse*, *District Lines*, *Hope and Heart Unite for ME/CFS Poetry and Art Slam*, *Forbidden Peak Press*, *District Lit*, *The Raw Art Review*, and elsewhere. It has been longlisted for the Palette Poetry Prize, shortlisted for *The A3 Review's* LOSING IT contest, selected as a quarter-finalist for the Nimrod Literary Awards, and chosen as a finalist for Public Poetry's Virus Anthology. Her writing is drawn in part from her degree in genetics from Cornell University, her ME diagnosis, and her interest in both art and science. Anderson plays in and co-directs a handbell choir, likes to learn new crafts including bookbinding and welding, and enjoys exploring the museums and side streets of her adopted city of Washington, DC. The poems in *Mellifluous*, a winner of the Uncollected Press Full Length Book or Chapbook of Poetry Contest, arose from her fascination with bees and her years keeping a Warré hive. While beekeeping, she discovered that she is allergic to bee stings. Now she admires honey bees' sunlit dances from afar.

www.ingramcontent.com/pod-product-compliance
Lightning Source LLC
Chambersburg PA
CBHW032110040426
42449CB00007B/1240